AF472220

# A MIXED BOUQUET

An Anthology of musings and poems

Ren Yaldren

First published in Great Britain in 2011
by
Farthings Publishing
SCARBOROUGH
YO11 2QB

www.farthings-publishing.com



My grateful thanks go to my friend and partner in Farthings Publishing, David Fowler, for all his help and encouragement in putting these musings together.

ISBN: 978-1-291-79288-1

Second edition: April 2014(b)

# CONTENTS

## MY GRANNY

My Granny was a sufferer-jet ( I think she flew a lot)
She revved her engines every day, it really made her hot.
Her throttle out, her mind in gear, all ready for some action.
Her squadron was the Women's Group (It was some sort of faction).

To battle! was my Granny's cry, (she always yelled a lot).
I was her child, she tutored me, I heard her in my cot.
Now I am grown and Granny dead, the faction is no more.
But in my dreams I see her now, flying off to war.

She would have loved the feminists, all fierce when they are young.
She would have burnt her bra and let her boobs go where they hung.
She would have marched, she would have fought and maybe gone to jail.
My Dad would have to cash his bonds, for money for her bail.

So keep it up my Granny dear, keep shouting from the ether.
I see you with your pinny on and written underneath 'er,
Is her own quote, I wrote it down, it makes my head go swimmin'.
"We want it now, we want it soon, we want the vote for women!"

# A REGIMENT OF TREES

A mountain range of fir trees.
Not an Everest or Matterhorn amongst them
Not even a decent sized hill.

Nature regulated by mankind, for its everyday use.
All wearing a uniform of tree green.
"Right dress you lot, you there, get in line
You at the end, you're too bushy – you need a haircut"
Said the Sergeant Major from the Forestry Commission.

Soon they'll be separated and holding up houses, or
Holding families, bottoms on chairs when they sit at table.
No time to phone home or send a photo, all leave is cancelled
Christmas approaches.

# REFLECTIONS IN THE ROSE GARDEN

Ravishing roses, proud monuments to Nature's miracles.
Each bed a community of colour, related by their harmonious hues.
Red, pink, yellow, peach, white, delicately blending together like
A Versace print.
Their scent is potent and heady, as I languish relaxed and alert.
In between them runs a motorway of green grass, soft without traffic.

A child feeds the society of pigeons; eager and fat they scramble for crumbs of Tesco's Value bread.
"Look Dad all those pigeons are eating bread!" exclaims one excited child.
"Mm" comes the reply, backed by years of indifferent aquaintance.
Pigeons are the pariahs of urban living, begging from strangers and sleeping rough.

One woman studies a crossword, "6 across, now let me see".
Another searches for words upwards, downwards, crossways, allways.
A squirrel shoots out then skids to a halt, one quick look and off he goes, disappearing like a phantom into the bushes.
No help there then – " 10 across..... " too absorbed to watch the drama at her feet.

Males are attempting to mate and puff out their chests and announce their intentions.
The females twist and turn in their attempts to get away and have a piece of the Value.
Nothing changes in Nature, males want sex, sex and more sex and women want Value.

The bench is hard and my back begins to protest.
One last look at the plethora of pigeons, whose lives are woven so inextricably with ours.
As I leave I realise that surrounding it all, is a perimeter of silence
Peaceful and persuasive, inviting me to return ere long.

# THE NIGHT SKY

Shining with binary precision they blanket the earth.
Regular, comforting, but largely ignored.

The mythical Gods play out their splendid tableaux;
Orion and Diana
hunters without parallel.

Nightly repeats.
No mousetrap this.
One ticket lasts a lifetime.

A tapestry of neon.
No Bayeux this, woven by Mathilda and her ladies.
The signature on this Masterpiece, is unknown.

# 10 BELMONT ROAD

Shabby genteel, a once proud monument to money.
Evoking a time when position and class, ruled.

Turreted walls proudly proclaim
An Englishman's home is his castle.

Enter in.  No fee to pay.  Just bills.

High ceilings and sweeping curves, command attention.
Provoking admiration, exclamation
"Wow this is wonderful."

Architecture to die for.  Not a cardboard box in sight.
Space!  Not the final frontier, but rooms to move in:
To spread your wings in.

Tall, elegant, with features to gawp at.
"Is that a Pre-Raphaelite window?"
Affirmative.  The experts say so.
Painted exclusively for the privileged owner.
Wealthy; church-warden; friend to famous painters
Morris, Burne-Jones, Rossetti.

Those were the days when friendships reaped rewards.
The price tag today – who knows!

# SWEET WILLIAM – IN HONOUR OF THE BARD

No one in the world can surpass you.
Words never failed you.
Heroes and Heroines.
Famous the world over.

Every actors dream.
To play the Dane, the Moor or Lear.
Kings and Queens.
Monsters and Saints.
You capture them all.

Your language is unique.
Riveting, descriptive, bawdy, magnificent.
No one can touch you
Except Marlowe.
A truly eloquent pair.

My poor efforts fail miserably
to capture the doomed lovers.
Romeo and Juliet.
Balcony bound.

Or Lear, the dysfunctional parent.
Demanding, not understanding.

Desdemona, reviled and killed
All because of a handkerchief.

A panoply of monarchs.
Vile, proud, strong, weak.
Get rid of the lot –
Bring on the Republic.

So said Caesar, but not Brutus and his pals.
They knew different.
He was a liar.
But Brutus was an honourable man.
So they say.

Beatrice got her Benedict.
There was Much Ado about Nothing.
Hamlet lost the lot.
So did Shylock.
All he wanted was a pound of flesh.

The Kings don't fair much better.
Richard Three; all he wanted was a horse!
Henry wanted wives.
He got six.
His lucky number.
Not theirs.

The Scottish play, full of murder, mayhem and magic.
Daggers and blood aplenty.
Ghosts make an entrance.
And an exit.
So does the Lady.

So does the Bear!

Who needs anything on their desert island, except
The Compete Works of William Shakespeare.

# FAIRIES

We have fairies at the bottom of our garden
I see them as they flitter to and fro.
One has a nose like Mr Jim Durante
And uses all the dock leaves in one blow.
They live inside a copper-bottomed kettle
Their entrance is the long and narrow spout.
Sometimes they visit all their elf relations
And leave a message saying 'We've gone out.'
It appears that no one else has seen these fairies
So reader of this warning you should heed.
It seems that smoking marijuana makes you
A fairy-seeing addict of the weed!

# FRUITS DE MERE

1. Of all the fishes in the sea The
mermaid is the fish for me. Well
actually that is not the case, I
prefer my fish without a face.

2. If you remove 3 octopus tentacles
You leave 5, like a pointed pentacle.
The octopus meanwhile isn't happy.
You'll get the ink, so make it snappy!

3. A crab moves sideways, what a hoot.
The weirdest creature when they scoot
And run away, their business pressing.
They don't want to end up with a dressing!

4. A ball of herring, what a sight.
All darting here and there.
In unison, to keep it tight
They could outrun a hare.
But dolphins are such clever chaps
All sly and working harder.
They fancy herring and are out
To stock up their fish larder.

5. Big ones, small ones, some as big as your hat.
Not coconuts, but fishes.
They swim around enjoying life
Then end up on our dishes.

# THE KISS

Iconic, famous, a wonder to behold
The Kiss by Gustave Klimt.
2 figures, wrapped in gold and love
Embracing.
Intimate for all the world to see.
He bends his head and cradles hers.
She turns her face to bare her cheek.
The Kiss is planted.

Colour erupts all around them;
Enfolding their bodies in a riot of shapes.
Hers are soft and round,
Evoking woman, soft and pliable.
His are harder; rectangles, black and solid.

She is kneeling. What of him?
He is an enigma, enveloped in a gold cocoon.
Head and shoulders emerge.
They bend and plant The Kiss.

His hands cradle her head.
Disembodied, they clasp her in a lovers' vice.
Her eyes are closed.
She could be dead.

## KUBHLA KHAN (with apologies to Coleridge)

In Zanadu did Kubhla Khan a stately pleasure dome decree.
He had 57 eunuchs and 2 virgins on each knee.
He loved to hear their voices and had formed his own sextet.
The virgins were the basses and the eunuchs the falsette.

“Come sing for me”, said Kubhla Khan, “a Londonderry air”.
The voices shrilled, the notes rang out and pigeons took to air.
He sat upon his throne so grand and marvelled at the sound.
Then rose up in his ecstasy, and fell upon the ground.

“The King is dead”, they all cried out, our singing was too much.
But truth to be, a eunuch had put oil upon his crutch.
Now eunuchs rule in Zanadu, no more are they a fiefer.
And Kubhla Khan is heard to cry, “you swines”, out from the ether.

# AN ODE TO THE HOTHOUSE FLOWERS**

I thought flowers had green stems?
Evidently not – these have pink limbs.

What is a hothouse?
A greenhouse for delicate blooms
Or an all Irish school in Dublin?

Do flowers make music?
Well bluebells chime and daffodils trumpet the arrival of Spring.
But these flowers sing a different tune.
They germinate the notes, nurture the growing song until suddenly
it erupts into blossom – helped by ample waterings of Guinness!

These are hardy annuals. They also transplant themselves into
foreign soil.
Glastonbury, Sidney, New Orleans.
An endless Garden Festival for enthusiasts.

I was a casual gardener. I cultivated exotic varieties –
A Domingo, Rachmaninov, a Chopin and a Verdi.
Then, my daughter scattered some new seeds –
A Liam, A Fiachnia and a Peter.
Soon they were established and outrunning all other varieties.

They are now so prolific that they are blooming everywhere –
even in the car!
They are colourful and vibrant.
I hope they bloom for a very long time.
They are so different in appearance – each one is unique.

I call them my Hothouse Flowers.

**(Hothouse Flowers are an Irish rock band who play great music. I first came across them in 1991.

# CANNED LOVE

It was a lowly council salt container
A sort of dirty yellow and all scuffed.
It longed to be an indoor shiny waste bin
And have a coat of polish and be buffed.
One day a kindly little girl aged 7
Was passing in her brownie uniform.
She gave the salt container a good cleaning
And painted on its lid in cuneiform.
It made the salt container look a picture
It looked and felt all very spick and span.
This poem really has a happy ending
Cos it found itself a shiny petrol can.

# REFLECTIONS

I oft reflect upon my life, the ups the downs the lonely way
I savour each reflective spot, where as a child I used to play
My friends and I so happy then, no hint of what our lives would bring
The pain the sorrow, tinged with joy, but always having time to sing
The children each, one girl one boy, ever changing, never dull
And then the devastating blow – “My dear we have been moved to Hull”.

# YET ANOTHER MILESTONE REACHED

'When I am an old woman I shall wear purple......' so said the poet Well, by the time you read this I shall be officially deemed to be an old woman, having reached my 60th Birthday in June! What doors will swing open for me, what offerings will I receive, as I wend my unsteady way down the rest of life's pathway?

Well actually, a heck of a lot more than I thought! Suddenly, from being one of the 'has-beens', I will have become one of the "do come in, let us make you welcome" brigade. Apparently we senior citizens are being courted as never before due to our burgeoning buying power. It seems that with property prices rocketing ever higher each year, and designer mortgages to match, everyone is so strapped for cash, that the only people who can afford to buy anything are us lot – the wrinklies!
All those trips to Peru, the canooing down the Orinoco, the backpacking trips to the base-camp at Mount Everest, the helicopter flights over Angel Falls, communing with the Amazon pigmies, are being booked up by those over the age of 55 and upwards – ever upwards! The mind boggles at corned-calloused feet being stuffed into the latest offering from Nike or Adidas; bodies staggering to the foot of Everest reeling on the latest walking poles from Berghaus. And why not I hear you cry!

When I look back I can see that we have been in the forefront of change for decades. We were the 60s Generation who invented pop-music, the Beatles, burnt our bras, took to drinking wine by the demijohn, stuffed flowers down the barrels of guns, wore the same flowers in our hair and danced half-naked at music festivals, called ourselves Ms, demanded equal rights with men (which we never got by the way), gave up knitting and sewing, and left home in droves! Ah yes, we were always ready to try anything once – well almost anything! Since then we have become grandparents but refuse to resume the knitting. We have become the SKIERS – Spending your Kids Inheritance!

Am I being selfish? Should I give in and sit down and await the arrival of the Grim Reaper? Is a free bus pass and a rail-card the height of ambition and sophistication?
Having got the fallen arches does this mean that my tramping days are over? Never!

So now that I am 60 and decidedly selfish, where shall I go? Well first of all I am off to Antartica with the chance to visit the hut – replete with actual artefacts – of Captain Scott and his ill-fated companions. Next is a trip to visit the volcanoes on the Pacific 'Ring of Fire', which is the most active volcanic area on the planet. After that a little trip around Iceland to see yet more volcanic activity. Then on to New Zealand for a 3 months sojourn in Middle Earth (for those of you who are Tolkien fans) and a chance to see whales in Kaikoura. After that a spot of sunbathing in Egypt before staggering up to base camp at the foot of Mount Everest, etc, etc.

So now that I am officially an old woman, who knows, I might even get myself a nice purple caftan and go on a pansy picking holiday to Costa Rica – I hear there are some rather nice old fossils to see there!

## OUT DAMN SPOT

What is that spot on yonder wall
Said Macbeth to his lady.
Tis nothing Sire, just Duncan's blood
Twill very soon be fadey.
What Duncan's blood! T'will never do
What if someone should bespy it?
Get out thy tool, remove the spot
With urine, that should dye it!

## THE FUNERAL

When you die, so I am told, they organise a 'do'
With sausage rolls and fairy cakes and wobbly jelly too.
With beer and wine and sandwiches and cream that comes from Devon
And where am I with all this food,
Sat starving up in heaven!

## MY GRANDAD – THE STAR PLAYER

Captured in a frame of black and white.
A young man, arms on hips, football style.
Medals on his chest proclaim his skill
Sutton United AFC 1908-9.
The Star Player.

2 large trophies proudly displayed at your feet
On upturned plant pots – who cares!
They prove your worth.
The Star Player.

You played your last game in World War 1.
At Ypres, against the opposing team.
You were killed.
The Star Player,

# THE BLACKSMITHS ARMS

Blacksmith's arms, the mind boggles
Muscles as hard as granite, wielding the hammer
Onto the anvil.
Sparks flying like coronal ejections, sizzling when they touch flesh.

He only makes horse shoes now, pots and pans are long gone,
Like the life in the smithy.
No skill in bashing a shoe, not when you've made a frying pan
Cast iron and solid like the Blacksmith's arms.

He's a sign now, over a pub, come in and buy one –
Or two or more.
Sparks also fly here, when tempers flare, like coronal ejections.

## THE MOON

There isn't much upon the moon, not even a nice beach.
There may be sand, there may be sea, but nothing we can reach. Its
grey they say and dusty too, you'd better wear your glasses You'll
also bounce, when walking there, wear weights strapped on your
asses.

It's not much fun, if you ask me, no bars to buy your booze in
Its freezing cold apparently, with gasses that are oozin.
So think again, it costs a lot, a vacation on the moon
We'll stick to Bognor. Postcard reads – we'll be seeing you all soon!

# FREE THOUGHTS
# WOMAN'S HOUR – AND NATURE

The tall tree has long thin leaves. They bend, bow and chatter, one to the other, exchanging talk.
'Birds again. They'll soon be making their nests.'

"She is up for the Man Booker Prize this evening. Tell me more about your poetry/"

The tree lower down has fat, broad leaves. It has long, stiff, branches, superior in their bearing. An officer, rather than an nco. They occasionally nod to each other.

"A survey of new mothers has found that 50% of them have no idea how much crying their child should do. Let us speak to an expert."
A man! What the hell does he know about new-born babies. Typical!
"Colic usually occurs in the early evening. We now believe we know what causes this. " I wait with baited breath for the oracle to speak.

"At 3 months the brain is changing. Babies discover that they can do things, such as smile, and it stops them from crying so much."
Is that it? I wonder how much that research cost? How do they know the brain changes at 3 months? Do they open one up and poke around? I am put in mind of the excellent definition of an expert.

An ex is a has-been and a spurt is a drip under pressure. Now a woman speaks.
"Try massaging your baby. We have found that gentle massage, especially around the abdomen area, helps to calm the baby down."
The trees nod. 'Yes, yes, we agree. You need to touch. Give love, affection, have patience. Everybody thrives on that – even trees.'
This is communicated with authority by a portly, medium sized tree, with long, erect branches.

“I have terriaki sauce, and soya sauce, and oh my God, I have 7 packets of beef gelatine. I can’t stop buying the stuff. I always imagine I am going to run out. I never have yet.”

The trees are perfectly still. Listening. ‘What’s cooking now?’ This from the tallest tree. It has to bend to hear what is happening.

“This would be great with mackerel or one of the other fatty fishes.”

It’s the serial now. Pop music background, played loudly at first.
“Stop. Police. This is PC204, I need assistance. A woman is herding sheep on Bethnal Green.
(cockney accent) What are you going to do Stacey, knit yourself a jumper?” Cockney accents, can’t abide them. They always sound so……..well, cockney!

The trees have lost interest now. They are standing perfectly still, minds switched off to Woman’s Hour. More interested in the comings and goings at the hotel next door.
‘Another coach arriving, says the birch tree. I wonder where it is from? Anybody heard the weather forecast?’

“What’s wrong with having sheep? They are a substitute for my Chloe. She was only a few months inside me, and they said she would never have lived, but I called her Chloe. I really wanted her.”

Never mind the trees, I’ve switched off. Of God, now it’s the obligatory West Indian mama. Hands on hips, ample bosom, wearing a bright coloured pinny.

(West Indian accent) “Why don’t you get yourself a dog girl? At least you can take it inside the house, and it don’t keep on making them noises.”

Back to the shepherdess. “Make sure the lambs are with the right ewes.”

Yee Gods, is this entertainment? Anything goes I suppose.

“If you want to know more about keeping sheep, go to our website at www.bbc.co.uk forward slash woman’s hour.”

The trees are nodding gently. Are they asleep?

## A NIGHT VISION
(apologies to Lord Byron)

She walks in beauty like the night
Wearing her see-through nightie
"It is the time", the soldiers cry
For this one she is flighty.
The soldiers shout, they love the sight
Their cheering is quite mighty.
Because the lady shows her charms
Not one time, but twice nightly.

## AN ODE TO VICTOR

Victor is a trusty steed, his wheels do turn and gather speed.
His driver sits in pride of place, a smile is always on his face.
He is well made and full of style
Pistons thrusting mile by mile. I
see it all from where I'm sat The
King of cars – Victor Passat
Understated elegance. A motor to be proud of.

# THE HUMPBACK WHALE

Mighty Leviathan
Loops and whorls map your skin.
Individual as fingerprints.

A graceful submarine,
painted from Nature's unique colour chart.

The tenor of the deep,
in an opera scored by time immemorial.

Your lunge; powerful, playful, awe-inspiring,
as you disappear with a flypast from your Vulcan of a tail.

Nature's naval patrol.

# MY HOSPITAL ODE

(written after visiting a friend in hospital).

"Oh t'was an awful time I had
In the hospital from hell.
I never got my drugs on time,
And I had to ring the bell.

The nurse she came and told me off
She saw my mobile phone.
I stuck two fingers up at her
And used it minus tone.

They left me feeling hot and ill
They even took away my pill.
I boiled and simmered till one day
My temper blew the fog away.

Where's my water? I did cry
The nurses seem to pass me by.
"I'm hot and sticky in my shirt
My bloody leg it don't 'arf hurt.

I fired my cannons full of shot.
They really did deserve the lot.
I'm fed up of being mucked about
Your incompetence has made me shout."

"Let's get rid of this old bugger,
He makes me want to be a mugger.
Let's pretend we want the bed
For someone who is nearly dead."

Now calm does reign where my friend is.
His bottle now has lost its fizz.
He is at home oh God be praised.
His leg he has to keep it raised.

"My leg will soon feel so much better.
I hope I don't become a fretter.
And as the weeks go slowly by
Bit by bit to walk will I.
Until the day when I am fit
To swim again and do my bit.
Back in harness will I be,
My ruddy health restored to me."

# THE GATHERING

Matthew was preparing a meal for some of his friends. He knew that they all liked their food, although they were not greedy. He had decided to use his largest table, so that they could all sit around it in comfort. One or two of them were quite well-built, and they liked to have plenty of elbow room.

He was planning a simple meal. There would be meat, cheese, olives, bread and plenty of fresh fruit. A simple repast, but one that was wholesome. He knew that several of his friends liked to drink wine, and he would ensure that there was plenty. It would not of course, be the best vintage. Those days were gone forever. Nowadays he had to make his money go a long way, as he was never very sure where the next wage would come from.

Matthew had once been a very wealthy man. He had been very clever in the pursuit of money, and was considered one of the brightest stars in the inland revenue. He was clever, and he always ensured that everyone paid the taxes that were due. No-one was allowed to get away with owing so much as one penny. He was the strong-arm of the department, and many people had received an unpleasant visit from him and his henchmen. Looking back, he knew that his methods were questionable, if not downright illegal at times. He could remember with distressing clarity the faces of many of his 'victims'. The pleading for more time, the crying and the screaming, when he removed their property in lieu of a bill they were unable to pay.

He had lived in a large house, with maids, a cleaner, and even his own chef. He ate sumptuous banquets several times a week, and all the best people in the town, clamoured to be one of his guests. He wore rich clothes, the best money could buy. He was not ungenerous. He used to pass on his clothes to his poorer cousins, when he tired of wearing them. Ah yes, those were the days – of wine and roses.

Then almost overnight it all stopped. His friends said he had had a terrible breakdown, and his mind was unhinged. He left his beautiful home, his luxury life-style and all his friends, and became a wanderer. His family and friends begged him to get treatment, to see reason, to come back home and resume his old life. But he could not. Something had happened to him, and he was changed forever.

His life was beggarly, his clothes shabby and unkempt. He tried to keep clean, bathing as often as he could, as he could never bear to be dirty. He wandered from place to place, sometimes getting a good reception and in others a violent one. He found himself in the company of other men, like him, who had dropped out of society and turned their back on the evil ways of men. They made a sorry bunch sometimes, but for the first time in his life he felt free. Yes, he, felt free, no doubt about it. Free from the responsibilities his money and possessions had placed on him. Free from the sycophants and hangers-on, whom he knew flattered his ego in order to get a free meal and a handout. Well no more. Despite all that he had gone through, he knew, in his heart, that life was truly good for him, for the very first time in his life.

He had finished setting the table, and stood back to admire his handy-work. Anything missing? No, it looked good. Plenty of food, but not piles of it. Just enough to ensure a good meal, amongst good company.

His guests began to arrive, and Matthew welcomed them in with a smile.
"Sit down my friends, help yourself to a drink of wine." The guests greeted each other and begun to chat together. They all knew each other very well, and felt comfortable in their familiarity. Finally the last guest arrived. He was a happy, smiling man, and he greeted

them all in turn.
“Where would you like me to sit Matthew?” he enquired.
“You are the guest of honour, so please will you sit at the head of the table Master.”
The man sat down and turned to one man who was still standing up, looking somewhat unsure as to where to sit.
“Come and sit by me Judas Iscariot.”

## MY TORTOISE

My tortoise falls asleep a lot, he has a lady friend.
He sits besides her every day, her lettuce he does tend.
They make some love, my mother says, but how I do not know
My tortoise has a tortoise shell, his girlfriend is called Flo.

We got a pet, for exercise, we hoped we would get fitter
My Dad he wished to walk a dog, when going for his Bitter
It's not much fun, to have this pet, he cannot talk or bark
The only exercise that we get, is to drag it round the park!

# OLD BIKES

We were travelling along on the road ‘cross the moors
Watching those who were hiking.
When all of a sudden a herd of old men
Shot past us, each one was a biking.
“They’re vintage old bikes” my driver exclaimed
“Old Nortons and some BSAs.
There’s Triumphs and Matchless and Royal Enfield
At school they were part of my essays”.
Oh those were the days when bikes were real bikes
And a sandwich was just called a butty.
No pizzas, no burgers, no big Macs or fries
And the beautiful game was called footie.
How nostalgic it is when the old bikes are out
We all start recalling old tales.
But was it good then, or is it best now?
Who knows, when your memory fails!

## THE NEW COMMITTEE

The Chairman sits before the Friends
The Minutes they must have amends
Each item slowly going through them
Will you and you say “I approve ‘em?”

Up shoot the hands, the Chairman smiles
He wants to work his cunning wiles
He wishes to appoint Committees
Whilst he will sit composing ditties.

“I have ideas, they are spot on, so listen whilst I spout.
You and you can be the ones to call the others out.”
We have to work to get results, so he can say three cheers.
He is the Chairman of the Bank and we are all cashiers!

# THE RITUAL

It's my turn now to choose a husband. My mother has instructed me in the finer points and I am very excited. The young men in the village all dress up and we the privilege ones choose. What am I looking for?

Well, let me see. He has to be very pleasing to the eye, beautiful even. That means he will have to be one of the specially reared clones. They are the genetically modified ones especially created for the women of the village.

I prefer mine over 6 feet tall. My sister's preference is the opposite. She likes to fondle her husband whilst looking him square in the eye.

I prefer mine with long hair so that I can run my fingers through it when we share intimate moments. It is also very useful in bringing him up sharp, should he ever consider stepping out of line.

Although we teach all our men to use our latest technology, my husband must be able to carry out designated manual tasks in the home. I know he will be happy to stand with his elbows in hot, soapy water, washing the dirty dishes. As an extra treat I will allow him to wash and scrub the dirty clothes – what could be more fulfilling?

He will need to be very obedient, as I can be a harsh task-master and a strict disciplinarian. However, I do not believe in deliberate cruelty and my bark is actually worse than my bite.

When I am ready, I will inform him of the need to procreate. He will perform the necessary function and then his work is done. His next nine months will be occupied in preparing the special bonding suite for our child and me. All the men are taught in school, those menial parenting tasks that need little thought, such as nappy changing. He will delight in indulging my every whim and when I wish to I will reward him. It goes without saying that he will be subservient to me, as all men are of course.

He will be allowed to have one evening each week, in which to meet with his friends. We encourage them to congregate together and provide ample outlets for their talents, such as furniture making, carpet weaving, cookery lessons, dressmaking. Some of them are even taught to read and write, but this is only in exceptional circumstances.

It is important for the women of the village to keep their brains alert and active. To this end we meet every week to discuss politics, philosophy, current affairs, financial matters, etc., in fact anything which any self-respecting woman in England would discuss.

Many amusing anecdotes are related at these meetings. One such is my favourite. We were informed, and the source seems to be a very reliable one, that many years ago, back in the dark ages, women in England were actually subservient to men! Of course we found it too incredible to believe and treated it as a joke. However, the source was adamant that the information was correct. It had been passed down through her family from Mother to Daughter for generations.

The Ritual is about to begin. I feel a slight twinge of nerves, but soon control these. For one brief moment I tried to imagine what it must have been like to be subservient to a man! Good God, the situation is too ridiculous to even contemplate!

# KING RICHARD'S CRY

"A horse, a horse, my kingdom for a horse."
The seatless King of England he did utter.
"Of course, of course, I'll furnish you a horse"
The farmer said on meeting with this nutter.

"I need it now so haste away,
I have to get me back into the battle.
So bring the beast, forget the feast
I wish to mount upon that sturdy cattle".

The horse looked up, he liked him not,
This seatless King of England with his armour.
The horse did bolt, so t'was its fault, that
The reigning King of England is a farmer.

## COME BACK DAD

### (Discussions in the nursery)

Our Dad has gone and left us
He got dressed and went off
He's gone to Castle Howard
He's acting like a toff.
Me and Gordon Bernard
Are sitting all alone
We haven't moved a muscle
We could be made of stone.
What if someone broke in?
What would we have to do?
I've only got me hat and scarf
To try to make them shoo.
I am a little fella
And Gordon Bernard too
Between us we can hardly
Raise enough sound to say boo!
So come back soon Dad come back
And give us both a cuddle
And then we won't feel we have
To get in bed and huddle
Under the big duvet which is so hot and black
We're pining for you our Dad
So do soon please come back!

# THE RELUCTANT PRISONER
## (More discussions in the nursery)

Our Dad is kept a captive
He hates it we all know
His temper is just simmering
But will soon start to blow.

We hear him in the morning
We hear him in the noon
If he does not get out of here
He'll murder someone soon.

He has a nasty virus
It has attacked his limb
It has gone red and swollen
But left the rest of him.

He cannot walk just hobble
He really is in pain
He wishes he were well now
Out walking in the rain.

So cheer up Dad we love you
We smile on you all day
And when you are asleep at night
We congregate and pray.

We want you to get better
We want you to go out
So we can see you smiling
And hear you sing and shout.

## TIPS FROM A CYCLIST

When cycling it is always prudent
To wear a helmet, like a student
One knock can send you really flying
The end result may be your dying!

## ROMEO AND JULIET

### (With apologies to Shakespeare)

What light upon yon window breaks, is it my Juliet?
Seated at her modem, sending emails on the net.

My heart doth flutter, with a sigh. I shrug and turn sway
But she remains, her fingers poised, dealing on Ebay.

## THE LARK ASCENDING

The Lark it is ascending
It's wings beat ever faster
I raise my gun, the deed is done
I shot it with my blaster.

## ODE TO A NIGHTINGALE

Your trill refrain is crystal clear
The tinkling of a bell
But as it's only 4am
I wish you were in hell.

## TO BE A TRAFFIC WARDEN

I want to be, when I grow up
A bossy Traffic Warden.
My father says they make him shout,
Especially Mr Gordon.

He waits each day when Dad alights
Advancing to the meter.
He reckons he was set on earth
To wrinkle out a cheater.

In go the coins, Dad hurries off
To work away all day.
He gets back late, his face all red
So Gordon makes him pay.

# THE REFRAINS OF SUMMER

Twas on a beauteous summer's day, a maid she was a walking
And on her shoulder dainty there, a parrot sat a squawking.
"Oh Pretty Polly hark ye now, why is it that you cry?"
Because the patch you put on me has covered my good eye!

^^^^

Now is the winter of our discontent made glorious summer
By global warming!

# WHAT'S IN A NAME

I know there are rumours about me. They are whispered in corridors, and amongst groups of people. Lurid rumours, that eddy around me like the tide. They say that I slept with my brother-in-law Franscesco. They say I committed the most cardinal sin of all with my father Alexander. My own father, who is the Holy Father to all the Catholics in the world. They even say that I let my brother Cesare into my bed. Will I always be talked about in this way?

I was first betrothed at the age of 10. I was still playing with my dolls and they gave me to the man 3 years later. It was 1493, and it was done to secure land and money for my family. I know this now, but at the time I was shocked to find myself expected to play happy families with an old, ugly wrinkled man. But Cesare got me out of it. He bullied my husband to say that we had not slept together and of course he had to agree. Everyone agrees with Cesare. He is cruel and ruthless, and no-one dare gainsay him. My second husband got on the wrong side of him, and Cesare had him suffocated. I was just a pawn in their games. I had no will of my own.

I have my faith though. The good sisters always allow me to retreat to their convent when the family conflicts become too much for me. When the fog of intrigue thickens so much that I think I am going to be choked by it. Then I ask God to help me. God helped me too, when I asked to be married to a kindly man, as my third husband. He was loving, and our relationship was a happy one. We both had lovers, as many couples do now, in this modern 16$^{th}$ Century. My lover is a poet, and of course there is always Franscesco. Not many people are as lucky as I am to have such a brother-in-law.

They say we Borgias are an unnatural family. Certainly, our father is the Pope, and as such is supposed to be celibate. But father always gets what he wants, and he wants power. More than anything else he wanted to become the head of the Catholic Church, and of course he got his wish. He is proud of his family, and even though he does not let us be seen always in his company – he has to maintain some outward show of compliance – when we are together as a family, he is a loving, devoted father. My brothers are ambitious and it suits them to have such a powerful father. Although Cesare is the second son, and destined for the church, he is the most powerful, and the most dangerous. As a child he used to test out poisons on animals, and sometimes on other children. He loves to watch people in agony, helpless and in great pain. We all know that no-one wants to be his enemy, and so he is indulged and feted as if he were Christ himself.

I often wonder what history will say about me, Lucrezia Borgia. Will I be remembered for my faith, and my love of solitude in the convent? Will I be remembered for the greatness of my father, Alexander Borgia, the Pope. Or will I be remembered for my brothers. For the deeds they do, which live after them, whilst the good is oft interred within their bones? Will I even be remembered or will I and all my family be forgotten? I wonder?

# DENMARK'S DOWNFALL

Goodnight sweet Prince, the bard did write
Of Hamlet when he snuffed it.
Ophelia dead, Polonius too,
My God how they had roughed it.

In Denmark it is really rotten
With Fortinbras out yonder.
Not many left, no King to rule
So who is left to ponder?

Young Fortinbras a Norway lad
Had always cast his eye on,
The State of Denmark and its crown
Was anxious he to try on.

Now Hamlet's gone, King Claudius too
Poor devils how they cried out.
No more sweet Prince, no more old King
The Dynasty has died out.

# THE STORY OF SPRING

I awoke from my long dreamless sleep. I always sleep deeply, as it allows me to rejuvenate myself and my magical powers. I need my powers, because the work I do involves a massive amount of effort on my part. I could not achieve what I have to do <u>without</u> having powers. It would be impossible.

My work only lasts for a very short time, but is so widespread and intense, that it is crucial to have had such a long sleep, in order to awaken 'powered up'.

My name is Spring. You will have surely heard of me. I am the entity who orchestrates the awakening of all new life around the world. When the winter equinox has passed and the amount of daylight lengthens, then I awake. The Sun announces the time by warming me, all over. I stretch every limb and exercise every muscle and sinew, until I am ready and prepared. Then I 'Spring' into action.

My touch gives life essence to all living things. I warm them, and their atoms begin to vibrate and dance with the joy of living. New life is created. A tiny bud pushes through the darkness. It calls out to the light " I'm here, look at me."

Creatures too feel my urgings. They begin to think about sex and procreation. They begin nest building. They only need a tiny part of my powers to awaken their own. The off they go, fully automated!

My joy is to give new life to all living things. I cannot arouse the dead. They leave the decay of old tissue and their spirits rejoin the Creator of all Life. There they rediscover life as pure energy. Totally indestructible.

My own life is very hectic. During the weeks, which I am flattered to find they have named after me, I do not rest. Neither day nor night. I fly at the speed of light, and anoint every living thing, with my magical power. Miracles happen all the time. These make me feel very good indeed. My job satisfaction is complete.

I am not unique. My brothers and sisters all around the world, also work their magic. The earth is a huge place and many of us are needed to carry out our Creator's miracles. They even work different shifts to me. When I return to my warm, dark bed, deep beneath the earth, they are just awakening. When my brother Winter blankets my home with cold and frost, they are emerging to bring Spring to other parts of the globe.

People say times change. I have noticed recently that the Sun has awoken me several weeks earlier than my usual time. This was a shock! However, I am very adaptable. With months of deep restorative sleep behind me, I can be up and ready for anything.

I like to hear my name mentioned. "Spring is here" they say. 'Springtime they call it.' "Put a Spring in your step." It is nice to know that when I make my appearance, people notice me, and feel better. I believe I am truly blessed to be Spring, don't you agree?

# NANNO NANNY

Forget me not!
Why not you cry?
I'm not in hell, nor in the sky.
My molecules are just much thinner.
I don't need clothes.
I don't need dinner.
My realm is at the nanno scale,
I've finally found the Holy Grail.

I'll watch you cry
I'll watch you caper.
You'll know I'm there, I'll write on paper.
No mystic Meg with psychic power
Will make you cringe
Or make you cower.

Your sense will feel warm and canny.
It isn't God.
It's Nanno Nanny!

# TREE LIFE

A Reservation of green tepees.
Made from cellulose and heated
through Nature's solar panels.

The Natives rise and greet the Sun,
turned on mechanically by its power.

Each tribe has its warriors;
guarding, foraging, fighting, killing.
Feet charging along the valleys of the trunk
Beating out the tomtom rhythm.

The scouts are alert to all danger;
Acid ready, to blind any intruder.
Food for the unborn, white, blind and deadly.

True communists in the making.

## NASAL DESIRE

Coco, Coco everywhere and not a drop to drink.
Because this is not from the bean, it is a pricey stink.
It costs a lot, a great deal more, than mortals can afford.
£50 for Coco Chanel. I get mine from abroad.

## COPPER HORSE INSOMNIA

I lay in bed a musin'
I should have been a snoozin'
The reason is the boozin'
I never should a choosin'

# EDWARD

Edward is a lofty bear, who is seated way up high.
He watches out and nods his head to seagulls flying by.
He is so introspective, he cogitates a lot
He muses on the clouds and knows it helps to stop the rot.

He came from far away to here, a big place known as Hull.
He was a gift to David and his heart strings he did pull.
He was a special present when David did reach 70.
He even went to Tuscany and felt he was in heaven-ty!

He has a happy home life, he gets a change of clothes.
Not many bears get such a treat with glasses for their nose.
He hopes to stay forever - it is a quite long time.
And one day he will write a book, that's if he has the time.

But until then he will look out and watch the world go by
Oh how he wishes he had wings he'd really love to fly.

## ROASTERS

Espresso, cappuccino, chocolate, skinny latte.
All these and more are sold in Roasters Café.
Ebony and ivory, Darjeeling and green tea
Will give you such a lovely shot, it is the place to be.

If you like good home cooking
Barrie is your man.
He is a whizz at breakfasts, a master with his pan.
The staff are really helpful, they greet you with a smile.
The Guardian rates them in top ten, of many and many a mile.

It is a little empire, with Barrie at the top.
The staff all rank below him, but really run the shop.
And now another venture, fresh food to take away.
The stuff to make you healthy, is made up fresh each day.

Scarborough needed Roasters to lift it to the top.
It is a town that's popular, but not a place to shop.
We hope they keep on trading for many a long year.
Let's hear it folks for Roasters, let's give them a big cheer.

# DRIVING

When I am behind the wheel,
my knees begin to knock.
I see the drivers rigid faced,
as stony as a block.
Men are the worst, such bad rapport,
must always have their way.
Its wacky races on the roads, I
see it every day.

They drive too close, they push and shove
their way in everywhere.
If you are waiting to move out
they look ahead and stare.
A gap, at last, has opened up
someone has let me out.
A woman driver, might have known
It makes me sing and shout.

Knights of the road, are women now
They truly are the best.
At leaving gaps and making life
Much better for the rest.
So watch out chaps and learn from us
The way to drive your cars.
And you will see that women are
The automotive stars!

# YOUR THOUGHTS

Take care with your thoughts
Lest those in spirit read them!
They do not stay within YOUR head
but are captured in the ether,
naked and exposed for all to read.

Imagine your thoughts composed in Neon,
A truly noble gas.
Flashing the words in Piccadilly Circus.
Cars crash, people gawp, open-mouthed at your vocabulary.
What colour are they – red, white or blue?
ALL is revealed!

So nurture them like your children.
Teach them how to speak –
nicely, courteously – obscenities are out!

Remember – children should be seen and not heard.

# BOUDICA

Boudica can bugger off!
She was too strong, she was too tough.
The Romans found they did not like her.
She fought them fierce, so they did spike her.

Her head it was displayed for all.
Beware of us or you will fall.
We are the Romans, you must fear us.
Keep well away, don't venture near us.

We will conquer one and all
So says the book – Decline and Fall!

# OUR OFFICE

A different atmosphere pervades our office.
No telephones ringing, people shouting
Mugs being rattled, voices piercing.

Concentration is our game.  We need it like a daily dose of statins.
Age cannot wither them – but the brain disagrees!
Use it or lose it.  That is certainly true.

People want to write and tell all.  Some tell more than all:
Secrets tumble out.  'Oops didn't meant to say that!
What will the missus say if she read it!'

Life is rich, full of mistakes, ambitions, joys and sorrows.
They put it all in.  We say nothing.  No comment.
Discretion is the better part of valour – mum's the word!

One sits typing, or playing – the whip gets cracked
'Get on with some work you!'
Head down, fingers racing over the keys.  Whew! I need a break.

We are getting there, slowly at first but now faster.
Commissions coming in and piling up.
Alas, we won't become tax exiles – will we ever make a profit?

## NOW'T SO QUEER AS FOLK – Written January 2014

People come in every size, with different hair and different eyes.
Their shapes they can be tall and slender, or shorter still and round and tender.
They eyes they differ when they're seen. Some are blue or grey or green.
Lots of folk have eyes rich brown: it makes no difference, all can frown.

Now hair that is a lofty subject. Some wear it long, a totem object –
Of fiery red or deep, deep black. They wear it down or sweep it back.
Blondes, they say, most men prefer. Marilyn Monroe, we owe this to her!
Yet men, they say, do marry brunettes: they much prefer them for their pets.

Well these days ladies, we can ring the changes. From blonde to black right through the ranges.
You mix the colour, shake it well – it might be liquid or even gel.
A splendid covering we can achieve; unless the colour makes you grieve.
'My God, I've got the colour wrong – and what is that disgusting pong?
I'll have to have another try – I can't wear this, I'd rather die!'

Now men , they say are at it too: with Grecian they can look like you.

I want a pair of boobs for Christmas! Or lift my face for special giftmas!
With help I can look like my daughter; with a cut of the knife
Like a lamb to the slaughter.

Was it better when all is said, to roll along to middle age spread?
Have batwing arms and double chins; a chocolate lover for our sins.
The pressure is to nip and tuck: the fat they can reduce and suck.
Well I for one ain't going that way; with lumps and bumps I'd rather stay.
Let gravity take all things south and lines can pucker round my mouth.

Life’s too short to worry needless – so I for one will live life heedless.
From this poem you can see, I poke the fun at you and me.
One thing I learnt, we have to joke.
‘Cos there is now’t so queer as folk!

## SHOES – Written January 2014

Where the hell did all these pairs come from?
I am sure they have grown and it didn't take long.
For boxes and boxes to appear in piles.
In some of them I have minced, in others walked miles.

Heels can differ depending on how I am feeling.
I can wear them flat or totter along near the ceiling.
The colours range across the spectrum –
I wonder where did I actually get them?

Ah! Yes, those were the ones that were a bargain;
Not to be missed, says the shoe sale jargon.
I counted them – that can't be right?
The total gave me quite a fright!

I will make a new year's resolution
To pare them down – that is the solution.
But what if I want them when once their gone?
They broke the bank – they weren't a song.

I think with hindsight I'd better keep 'em
No regrets and no bouts of weepin'.
Now that I've sorted out my toots
I'd better start and count my boots!!

## SCARBOROUGH TOWN – Written January 2014

The world's first seaside town is Scarborough.
It has 2 beaches, a pier and harbour.
A woman found some healthy water,
So folks did flock – not poor but haughter!

They built grand houses, some were mansions,
Great big doors and fancy stantions.
Servants came to wait and flutter,
Their every whim, their every utter.

A stroll along the golden beach;
The carriage made it within reach.
The Esplanade, well that came later,
But strolling there, well that felt greater.

With parasols up high, erect;
Just look at us, we are select.
We look at you and raise our noses:
Good job we can inhale our posies.

The railways put a stop to that.
They brought those with a working hat.
They came along in all their thousands,
So up went lots of boarding houses.

The toffs they were put in a state,
With hoi polloi we will not mate!
Scarborough now we all do hate
So it's off to Harrogate!

## EE BY GUM – Written after a particular horrendous visit to the dentist, March 2014

Teeth! Now there's a topic to set us all chattering.
From arrival to leaving they're given a battering.
When we are born we're all nice and gummy.
It's nature's way of protecting our mummy.
Then one by one the teeth poke out
It's when we learn to scream and shout.

The first set are small, but fairly robust
They give us the feeling that we really must –
bite the cat's tail or bite the dog's ear.
In fact we'll sample whatever comes near.
Sometimes that is a person who'll coo.
Who offers a finger they want us to chew.
The sounds that they make when being bitten –
Why! It's more fun than sucking a mitten!

Then in a few years these teeth start to fall out
The tooth fairy comes and her gift makes us all shout
A pound! What a thrill, we find 'neath our pillow.
"It were sixpence in my day" I hear Grandad bellow.

The new teeth arrive, with re-spon-sibility.
They need lots of care and lots of agility.
You only get one chance this time, not two.
The care of this set is just up to you.
We pound them each day with a much varied diet
We eat lots of food and others we'll try out
Some of it's good and some of it's sweet.
The latter we think of as having a treat.

But woe betide us, in a state compos mentis
If we find our teeth need a trip to the dentist!
This visit's a nightmare, whilst we are still waking
And leaves us like jellies, all wobbly and shaking.
The room has appearance of all instrumental
The sound of the drill leaves us all feeling mental!
"Open wide please" a quick poke and a prod.
You can't say a word, you just give a nod.

A flow of talk comes, all of a tumble
Your mouth is full up, allows only a mumble.
And finally after, what seems like a lifetime
It's over at last and now it is high time –
to give up the treats that are sticky and yummy.
Or else face the future with your mouth all gummy.

The moral my friends, of my little story
Is teeth and the subject of, can be quite gory.
They hurt when they first make a junior entrance.
A lifetime of use; it can be quite a sentence
Of pain and distress, not least when they're leaving
Our bosoms they can leave us crying and heaving.
So be warned when treats, with your conscience clashes
We all need to make sure we cherish our knashers.

## CATS - Written March 2014

Cats are the animals that I really love.
To me they are sent as a gift from above.
They give me a thrill when I stroke them
I never would prod or would poke them.

They come in all shapes and all sizes.
Their markings are often disguises.
The tiger, a beast of such grandeur
To cats whose size makes them much handier.

To keep as a pet for a lifetime.
Getting one, it's always the right time.
The pleasure they give you is endless.
You'll never end up feeling friendless.

They can't be taught lessons or tricks, mind
<u>They</u> decide when their fun they'll find.
It's usually at night when we're sleeping
They have a routine and go peeping.

Across the lawn they go a'stalking
Without any chatter or talking.
The hunter within has been woken
They'll leave you a positive token.

Just where they know you will find it
You have to make sure you don't mind it.
Cats prove that nature is raw
They demonstrate with tooth and claw.
But don't let that part make you fussy.
You'll get joy and delight from a pussy!

## BIRD TALK - Written March 2014

Whilst working one day in my garden
A bird it hoped up and it said
“Good morning, do you have some bird seed?
We’re rather fed up with the bread.
It makes us all heavy and bloated
When we are supposed to be floated.
We peck and we fill up our crops
Whilst over your garden we hops.
If into our crops we do cram it
It doesn’t help aero-dynamics.
Our wings have to beat that much faster
Or else taking offs a disaster!
So please will you get us some bird seed?
It is what we like and what we need.
I do hope you will beg my pardon.”
And off he flew out of the garden.

## MABEL ON THE TABLE

An amazing piece of hardware sits snuggly on my table.
It is a modern computer, all shiny black, called Mabel.
Although it is called Mabel, it really is a fella
With buttons proud and solid, just press one it will tell'y
You can do wonders with it and even surf the net.
It's full of fancy programmes I haven't figured yet.

We all now know of Google, a strange but famous name.
In over just a decade it has rocketed to fame.
We could not do without it; they've put in in the movies.
You see them pressing Google; it makes them look like smoothies!
I personally like to surf the net, it makes me feel so free.
We really must give all our thanks to Sir Tim Berners-Lee.
How did we do without them? Our lives were so much harder.
If you hate shopping you can order stuff to stock your larder.

You needn't move from sofa, give it a fancy font.
With just a click on Amazon you can order what you want.
So let us cheer the progress, computers give our lives.
It means we can stop speaking to our husbands or our wives!
Anyone can use them, it covers all the ages.
From children barely talking, right through to ancient sages.

So if you don't possess one you really ought to ponder
The wonders it will open, the places you can wander.
I never want to lose mine, I use it every day.
I have so many games on it I can spend hours at play.
It has become a habit I never want to break
Hip hip hooray for Mabel and the pleasure you do make!

www.ingramcontent.com/pod-product-compliance
Ingram Content Group UK Ltd.
Pitfield, Milton Keynes, MK11 3LW, UK
UKHW041918190726
13854UKWH00003B/1311